# The Lewis and Clark Expedition

Written by Sanna Porte Kiesling

Illustrated by Dan White

TWODOT

*Dedicated to Dick & Neva Porte,*
*who taught me to love adventure.*

**A TWODOT BOOK**

Copyright © 1990 by Falcon® Publishing, Inc., Helena, Montana
A division of Landmark Guidebooks, Inc.

Design, illustrations, typesetting, and other prepress work by Falcon,
Helena, Montana. Printed in Hong Kong.

Library of Congress Number 88-083881

ISBN 0-937959-60-X

# A Blank Spot on the Map

In May 1804, a group of young men stepped off the edge of civilization and launched one of the most amazing adventures of all time. They planned to travel the Missouri River upstream to its source, more than two thousand miles away from their launching point near St. Louis, in what is now Missouri. They would then try to cross the Rocky Mountains, find the mighty Columbia River, and float down it to the Pacific Ocean. If they survived that far, they would have to make their way home again.

If you can imagine being the first to explore an unknown galaxy today, you'll understand what kind of trip these men faced in 1804. They knew almost nothing about the wilderness they would enter. It was a great mystery—a huge blank spot on the map. There were rumors that giant prehistoric monsters and fire-breathing dragons roamed that country. For most of the trip the men would be in land no white man had ever seen. They would have few maps to follow— no guide except their wits, their instincts, and occasional information from Indians.

Everything the men needed to survive for two years would have to be found, made, or carried in their small wooden boats. There were no airplanes to fly in extra supplies, and there were no stores in which to buy them. They had no doctor and no way to get help in an emergency. But they did have two very brave and intelligent leaders. Their names were Meriwether Lewis and William Clark.

# The Race Is On

"Captain Lewis?" The soldier saluted as he entered the office of President Thomas Jefferson's personal secretary. "The president wants to see you, sir." Meriwether Lewis strode quickly to the president's office. Jefferson was studying a large parchment map.

"Come in, my friend," the president said. "I have some interesting news." He leaned back in his leather chair. "Do you remember all our talks about exploring the continent and finding a water route to the Pacific Ocean?"

"Of course, sir," Lewis said. "It's my fondest dream to find such a route."

Jefferson nodded. "My dream, too, and the dream of every New World explorer since Columbus—to find a Northwest Passage. The British have the same dream. So do the Spanish and French. The British make me especially uneasy," he continued. "Their man Alexander Mackenzie came very close to finding a route across Canada to the Pacific—too close. You know what it means if the British find a route before America does."

Lewis knew, all right. It meant bad news for America. The British fur companies would have a faster, easier way of getting their furs to the Pacific Coast. From there, they could ship them to the rich markets in China. If the British controlled the fur market, they would

rule the whole northwest part of the continent as well. That would threaten America's settlement of the West.

"We must find a route first," Lewis said.

"Exactly," Jefferson replied. "And that's my news. Congress has just agreed to provide the money for an expedition to the Pacific. I want you to lead it."

Jefferson excitedly traced his finger along the map. "I'm convinced that you could follow the Missouri River to its source in the Rocky Mountains—wherever they may be. Find a low point in the mountains where you can cross. Then find the Columbia River and follow it to the Pacific Ocean."

The president looked back at Lewis. "I want you to learn everything you can about the geography, plants, animals, and Indian tribes along the way. But above all, find a route, Lewis. Find it before the British do."

# Partners in Discovery

To help him lead the expedition, Lewis chose one of the bravest men he knew—his friend, William Clark. Clark was living in Kentucky when he got Lewis's invitation to join the great adventure. He lost no time in replying. "My friend," he wrote, "I join you with heart and hand."

And so one of the most remarkable partnerships in history was formed. In some ways, 29-year-old Lewis and 33-year-old Clark were as different as two people could be. Tall, lanky Lewis was a solemn man, quiet and often withdrawn. Red-headed Clark was talkative, outgoing, and jolly. Yet they had many things in common, too. Both men came from well-known Virginia families. They had served together in the army on the frontier, where they had learned to survive in the wilderness. Both were very intelligent.

Technically, Lewis was the leader of the expedition. Clark was supposed to be second in command. But Lewis knew the value of teamwork. He insisted that Clark share equal rank with him. The two captains made all major decisions together. One of the few things they disagreed on during the trip was the taste of dog meat. Clark hated it. Lewis thought it tasted pretty good, especially after a steady diet of dried berries.

These two men, who stayed friends for life, worked together in perfect harmony. If either had ever insisted on his own way, the expedition might have failed.

# Preparing for Adventure

As Lewis got ready to leave Washington to begin the great adventure, surprising news reached President Jefferson from Paris. Napoleon, France's ruler, had decided to sell the French territory of Louisiana to America for fifteen million dollars. So America now owned the whole western drainage of the Mississippi River—almost all the land between the Mississippi and the Rocky Mountains.

When he heard this news, President Jefferson gave Lewis more instructions. "This Louisiana Purchase puts a new light on your expedition, Captain Lewis," he said. "It appears that most of the land you'll be exploring is within Louisiana. See if you can find out how big the territory is and what's out there. Also, you had better explain to whoever lives in Louisiana that they live in the United States now."

From December 1803 to May 1804, Lewis and Clark camped near the mouth of the Missouri River and trained their men. Captain Clark had brought with him nine Kentucky volunteers, all of them strong mountaineers and good hunters. He had also brought his black servant, York. In addition, the captains had recruited sixteen U.S. Army soldiers. Two of them, Peter Cruzatte and Francis Labiche, were experienced French rivermen. Lewis and Clark had also hired an interpreter named George Drewyer who knew Indian sign language. Several more soldiers and rivermen would travel with the main group as far as the Mandan Indian villages in what is now North Dakota. With Lewis's big Newfoundland dog, Seaman, the crew of about forty-five was complete.

When spring arrived, the explorers began loading their boats. Lewis had designed a 55-foot-long keelboat with a square sail and 22 oars. It would be accompanied by two flat-bottomed boats called *pirogues*. Into these boats, the men loaded rifles, kegs of gunpowder, fourteen barrels of cornmeal, twenty barrels of flour, seven of salt, and fifty of pork. Then they loaded bundles of beads, belts, pipes, kettles, mirrors, U.S. flags, and medals stamped with a picture of President Jefferson. Lewis and Clark hoped these presents would help win the friendship of the Indians. But just in case, they fixed three small cannons onto the deck of the keelboat. The expedition had strict orders from President Jefferson to avoid fighting with the Indians. Still, Lewis and Clark thought the guns might come in handy if they needed to impress the natives.

Finally, on May 13, every last crate and box had been loaded.

That night, seventeen-year-old George Shannon couldn't sleep. He was too excited, for tomorrow the adventure would begin. He sat up in his bedroll and looked over at Sergeant Nathaniel Pryor, who was writing one last letter home.

"What do you think, Sergeant?" Shannon said. "Could the Rocky Mountains really be as big as the Indians say, so high they reach the sky?"

Pryor shrugged. "You can't believe every story that gets passed from tribe to tribe all across the prairie. The president thinks we can cross the mountains in half a day. I hope he's right. Anyway, it's months before we have to worry about that. I'm content to worry about my scalp for now."

# The Adventure Begins

On May 14, 1804, the explorers launched their boats into the wide, muddy Missouri River. They sailed and rowed upriver to the French village of St. Charles, where they stopped to buy last-minute supplies. As the expedition left St. Charles, a handful of villagers came to the riverbanks to cheer them.

The expedition moved slowly against the Missouri's swift current. The men had to stay alert for sandbars and crumbling riverbanks. One night, Clark woke up and noticed that the riverbank above their boats was about to collapse. "All hands on!" he yelled. The startled men grabbed their gear, leaped into the boats, and pushed away from shore just before the bank crashed down. Had it fallen a minute earlier, it would have sunk the boats.

In late August, Lewis and Clark met their first Indians, members of the Oto tribe. The captains gave presents to the Oto chiefs and told them they now had a new Great Father who lived in Washington, D.C. They explained that the Great Father wanted them to live in peace with American traders. The explorers would deliver the same speech to every Indian tribe they met on the trip.

During the meeting with the Otos, two soldiers decided they'd had enough of the trip and ran away. One escaped, but the other, Moses Reed, was caught and punished. He had to run four times through a double row of soldiers while they hit him with switches—a punishment known as running the gauntlet.

Soon after that incident, young George Shannon disappeared. But he hadn't run away. Shannon had been hunting on shore and had stopped for a rest. He woke up thinking the boats had passed him, and he raced to catch up. He spent two weeks alone, living on wild grapes and a rabbit that he killed with his last bullet. Finally, he gave up trying to catch the boats. He started walking downstream, hoping that a fur trader would float by and give him a ride to St. Louis. Suddenly, he saw the keelboat coming upstream! The expedition had not passed him after all.

This near-disaster was followed by real tragedy. Sergeant Charles Floyd began to suffer from terrible stomach pain. Lewis tried giving him pills and powders, but the sergeant died, probably of a ruptured appendix. Miraculously, he was the only person to die during the expedition.

In September, the party met a band of Teton Sioux warriors. Lewis and Clark had heard about these fierce Indians. The Sioux had all but closed the Missouri to white traders coming upstream from St. Louis by robbing each passing boat of its goods.

The captains gave the Sioux their usual speeches and handed out the usual gifts. Then they took the chiefs aboard the keelboat. They hoped that a gun demonstration would impress the Indians. But when Clark took the chiefs back to shore in a pirogue, several warriors grabbed the pirogue and threatened to hold Clark hostage unless they got more gifts. Clark had to think fast. Should he draw his sword and call their bluff? What if they weren't bluffing? Clark drew his sword. Instantly, the Sioux yanked arrows from their quivers.

"Hold it!" came a shout from the keelboat. The Sioux turned to see Lewis and his men pointing guns at them. After a long pause, the warriors lowered their bows and Clark rowed away unharmed.

If the captains had shown any weakness or fear, the Sioux probably would have run them off the river—or even killed them. Instead, Lewis and Clark remained calm, firm, fair, and honest. These qualities were to earn them the respect of Indians all across America.

# Winter among the Mandans

In late October, the men arrived at the villages of the Mandan Indians, about sixty miles north of where Bismarck, North Dakota, is today. There they held a council with the Mandans in one of the Indians' big dome-shaped earth lodges.

Like other Indians the expedition met, the Mandans had never seen a black person like York before. They were fascinated. They thought York was really a white man painted black. They tried to rub the "paint" off. York found this very funny. He made them even more curious by pretending to be a ferocious wild animal.

After the council, the explorers began building Fort Mandan—eight cabins in which to spend the winter, surrounded by tall, pointed posts. The Missouri would soon freeze, ending travel until spring. As the men fitted logs into place, a French-Canadian trader named Toussaint Charbonneau arrived. He had heard about the expedition and had come looking for a job as an interpreter. With him was his pregnant sixteen-year-old Indian wife, Sacagawea.

"Tell him we could use someone who speaks the Hidatsa language," Lewis said to Labiche. "But we can't have a woman slowing us down." The riverman repeated Lewis's words in French.

"Listen," Charbonneau replied, "my wife is a Shoshone from the mountain country. The Hidatsas kidnapped her as a child and sold her to me. If you plan to cross the Rocky Mountains, you will need to buy horses from the Shoshones. I don't speak Shoshone, but she does." When Labiche translated this, Lewis looked at Sacagawea with sudden interest. "You're hired," he told Charbonneau.

The expedition moved into Fort Mandan just as the first winter blizzards came shrieking across the prairie.

At daybreak on December 25, 1804, the men woke their captains with a Christmas salute. They sang carols and fired the cannons into the frosty air. "Merry Christmas!" they shouted as the captains came out of their cabins. "A drink of rum all around!" a laughing Clark shouted back. The explorers drank a toast to the health of President Jefferson as John Colter raised the American flag.

Then Peter Cruzatte got his fiddle and played a jig. The men danced. Sacagawea watched the festivities with wide-eyed wonder. She couldn't understand the men's behavior. "This is a big medicine day for us," Drewyer explained in sign language. When the dancing and feasting finally ended that night, the men drifted to sleep thinking of their families and friends at home, so many miles away from that frozen, lonely prairie.

The explorers kept busy during the long winter. While the men hunted, stitched new elkskin clothing, and hacked dugout canoes from tree trunks, Lewis and Clark wrote detailed reports to President Jefferson. They described the Indian tribes they had met, explaining their customs and languages. They also described the new and strange animals they saw on the prairie. They had seen prairie dogs, pronghorn antelope, mule deer, coyotes, and bighorn sheep. But they had not yet met the West's most dangerous animal, the grizzly bear. The Indians had told them tales about the ferocious beast, but the explorers thought these stories were exaggerated. "I imagine a grizzly might be pretty fearsome if you only have a bow and arrow," Lewis said. "But they'll be no match for a modern rifle and gunpowder." He would soon learn differently!

One day in February, when the expedition's thermometer read 42 degrees below zero, a new arrival came to Fort Mandan. Sacagawea gave birth to a dark-eyed baby. His father named him Jean Baptiste, but to his mother he was Pomp, "firstborn" in Shoshone. He became the youngest member of the Lewis and Clark Expedition.

# From the Mandan Villages to the Great Falls

Spring finally began thawing the ice-bound Missouri. On April 7, about a dozen of the party boarded the keelboat and started back to St. Louis. With them, they took reports, maps, antelope skeletons, mountain sheep horns, and live prairie dogs.

Lewis, Clark, and the remaining explorers, as well as Charbonneau and his family, turned their boats upstream. The expedition now faced the most dangerous part of its journey. It must cross an expanse of wilderness more than a thousand miles wide. No one knew exactly what lay ahead, but spirits were high. Lewis and Clark had carefully chosen only the strongest and best men to continue the journey. They had sent Moses Reed and other potential troublemakers home. "The party are in excellent health and spirits," Lewis wrote in his journal. "All act in unison, and with the most perfect harmony."

Within a few weeks, the expedition reached the land that someday would be called Montana. There Captain Lewis learned proper respect for the grizzly bear.

The explorers killed their first grizzly near where Culbertson, Montana, is today. It was a young bear, weighing only about three hundred pounds. Lewis shot it easily. He was convinced that the Indians had exaggerated the bear's savagery.

But not long afterward, the party encountered a full-grown, six-hundred-pound grizzly. It charged the men like a runaway train.

Ten bullets were needed to kill it, and even then the bear swam across the river and roared horribly for twenty minutes before it died. A few days later, some of the party's best hunters fired seven bullets into a grizzly. The angry animal still chased them into the river. "These bear being so hard to die rather intimidates us all," a humbled Lewis wrote in his journal. "I must confess that I do not like the gentlemen and had rather fight two Indians than one bear."

The explorers had close calls with wildlife almost daily—and not just grizzlies. One night a bison charged through camp. Lewis's dog, Seaman, began barking wildly. This terrified the bison into a frenzy. What an uproar! The bison came within inches of trampling some of the sleeping men before Seaman finally chased it out of camp.

On another occasion, Lewis was charged by a grizzly, a wolverine, and three bison—all in one day! He was also nearly bitten by a huge rattlesnake. "It . . . seemed to me that all the beasts of the neighborhood had made a league to destroy me," he wrote.

In June the expedition reached a point where the Missouri seemed to divide into two rivers the same size. Which was the real Missouri and which was a tributary? If the expedition followed the wrong river, it would lose weeks of precious time. The captains decided to explore farther on foot. Lewis took some men up the northern river, which he named Maria's River after his cousin, Maria Wood. Today it's known as the Marias. Clark and several others examined the southern river.

When the two scouting parties returned to base camp, everyone was convinced the northern river was the correct route—everyone except Lewis and Clark. "We'll follow wherever you lead," Sergeant Pryor told the captains. "You haven't led us astray yet. But the northern river looks like the right choice to me."

"We can't afford to make the wrong choice," Lewis replied. "I'll explore the southern river further."

After a couple days of exploring the southern river, Lewis noticed a tremendous roaring sound. He followed the sound to a series of five thundering waterfalls. Lewis was jubilant. He knew now that this was the true Missouri, for the Hidatsas had told him about these great falls. Lewis later described the falls as "the grandest sight I ever beheld."

"The southern route is the right one!" Lewis told the men when he returned to base camp. "I found the great falls. Now we just have to figure out how to get around them."

# To the Three Forks

It took two long, agonizing weeks to get boats and baggage around the great falls of the Missouri. The men had to build rough wooden wagons, slicing a tree trunk to make crude wheels. They loaded their boats and supplies onto the wagons. Then they strapped on harnesses and began shoving and pulling their burden eighteen miles up a steep, rocky hillside and over the rough prairie.

Bloodthirsty mosquitoes, burning heat, grizzly bears, and violent storms kept the explorers steady company during this portage. One day a sudden storm pelted them with hailstones big enough to knock them down. Another day, Clark and the Charbonneau family almost drowned in a cloudburst. They had been walking along the Missouri when the storm hit. Afraid that the raging wind would blow them into the river, they crouched under some overhanging rocks in a ravine. Suddenly they saw a torrent of flood water pouring down the hill. It headed straight for them, tearing up rocks in its path. They barely had time to scramble out of the ravine before it filled with water fifteen feet deep!

Finally the portage was completed. The exhausted explorers put their boats back into the river above the falls. Once broad and muddy, the Missouri now ran clear and wild. The men often had to get out and tow the boats, wading up to their armpits in water that got colder as they drew closer to the mountains. Their boots had long since worn out, and they had only thin moccasins between their feet and the cactus that carpeted the prairie. Cactus and sharp river rocks had cut and bruised their feet so badly that some could hardly walk.

On July 19, the party passed through a narrow canyon where dark cliffs towered above the river. Lewis named these cliffs the "gates of the Rocky Mountains" because they seemed to open like giant gates, leading the explorers into the mountains. Today, visitors can still experience this sensation at Gates of the Mountains just north of Helena, Montana.

Lewis and Clark were anxious now to find the Shoshone Indians. They needed to buy horses from the Shoshones to cross the mountains that loomed ahead. If they were to get over the mountains before heavy snows came, they would have to find the Shoshones soon. In that high country, heavy snows could fall as early as August.

The captains had seen signs of Indians along the shore, so they knew they were being watched. But the Indians remained hidden. "They probably think we're a war party," Lewis told the men. "Let's keep the flags flying over the boats. At least they'll know we're not Indians. Maybe they'll understand that we come in peace."

But still no Indians appeared. One day Clark drew Lewis aside. "This is getting desperate," he said. "It's nearly August. We've got to reach the Shoshones. I'll take a few men and start walking overland. It'll be faster than fighting this blasted current with the boats."

Lewis looked down at his partner's feet. They were bleeding from

the sharp rocks and cactus. He shook his head. "Your feet...,"
he began.

Clark stopped him. "Nobody else's feet are in any better shape.
Anyway, I'd rather tear them up a little more than freeze them off.
And that's what'll happen if we don't get over the mountains before
the snow falls." He hoisted his pack over his shoulders. "I'll wait for
you once I reach the three forks Sacagawea talks about."

Within two days, Clark and his men came to a place where three
rivers poured out of the mountains to form the Missouri. Clark was
sick with fever and chills, but he was determined to find the
Shoshones. He kept walking, exploring the three forks. No Shoshones.
Finally, nearly delirious with fever, he trudged down the middle fork
to find that Lewis had arrived at the three forks with the canoes.

That night the worn-out explorers camped at the three forks of the
Missouri. They were almost 2,500 miles from St. Louis. Sacagawea
recognized the campsite as the exact place where she had been
kidnapped as a child. "She says the Shoshones can't be far away,"
Charbonneau told the captains.

"I hope to God she's right," muttered Lewis grimly. "We are
running out of time."

# The Search for the Shoshones

On July 30, the expedition started up the northernmost of the three rivers, which they had named in honor of President Jefferson. The Indians had told them that this river would take them west. Progress was slow on this swift, rocky stream. It got narrower as it wound higher into the mountains. Finally there was no room to paddle. The men had to pull the boats upstream, wading in the icy water. To make matters worse, game was scarce in these mountains. The men had to do their backbreaking work on little food. Half of them were sick. Their good cheer finally began to wear thin.

On August 9, Captain Lewis took off on foot with George Drewyer, Hugh McNeal, and John Shields to look for the Shoshones. "We're not coming back until we find them," Lewis vowed, "even if it takes a month." For three days, Lewis and his men followed a faint set of horse tracks. Finally they sighted a lone brave on horseback, but the Indian rode off before the white men could talk to him. "Disaster," thought Lewis. "He'll ride straight to his people and warn them to run away." There was nothing to do but follow the Indian's trail.

The horse tracks followed a stream up a mountainside. When the stream ended at a spring, Lewis turned to his companions. "This is it," he said. "The birthplace of the Missouri River."

The men went on over the ridge, entering the present state of Idaho. On the other side, they found a stream flowing toward the setting sun. Flowing west! They had reached the backbone of the continent, where the Continental Divide separates east-flowing rivers from west-flowing rivers. At some point, this stream would flow into

the Columbia River, and the Columbia would lead them to the Pacific Ocean. But first they must cross the snowcapped mountains that stretched ahead as far as they could see. The search for the Shoshones continued.

The next day, the men met three Indian women on the trail. One woman ran away in terror. The others sat with their heads in their arms and waited to be killed. Lewis gently took the older woman's trembling hand. He said the word Sacagawea had taught him: "Tab-ba-bone. White man." He pulled up his sleeve to show his white skin, for the sun had tanned his hands and face as dark as any Indian's. When the old woman saw this, she raised her head in astonishment and looked into Lewis's blue eyes. She didn't know what a white man was, but at least she knew he wasn't an enemy.

Using sign language, Drewyer asked the women to lead them to the Shoshone camp. On the way, they met sixty Shoshone warriors on horseback. Lewis dropped his gun and held up an American flag. His heart pounded. The success of the expedition hung by a thread now, and so did their lives.

One of the warriors, a young chief, exchanged words with the women. Then he dismounted, laid down his spear, put his arm around Lewis's shoulder, and pressed his painted cheek against Lewis's cheek. "Ah-hi-e," he said. It meant, "I am much pleased." Lewis sighed with relief.

Lewis led the Shoshones back over the Divide to meet Clark and the rest of the party. Clark's group had been moving slowly up the Jefferson, wondering whether their friends were dead or alive. All at once Clark saw Sacagawea jumping up and down, sobbing and

15

laughing at the same time. She had seen the Shoshones approaching with Lewis, and she recognized them as the very band from which she had been kidnapped. Tears streaming down her cheeks, she sucked her fingers, which meant, "These are my own people, among whom I was nursed."

Sacagawea explained the expedition's need for horses to the Shoshone chief, Cameahwait. Suddenly she recognized him as her own brother! She threw her blanket over Cameahwait's shoulders and burst into tears. She was so shaken with emotion that she could barely translate.

The Shoshones agreed to sell twenty-nine horses to the explorers, but Cameahwait warned them that the only route through the mountains was very dangerous. The Nez Perce Indians used that route, he said. It crossed rugged country where few game animals lived. The explorers might starve.

"If the Nez Perce can make it through," Lewis said, "so will we."

# Across the Rocky Mountains

On August 18, Lewis spent his thirty-first birthday making pack saddles for the trip across the mountains. The explorers filled their boats with rocks and sank them in a pond near the head of the Jefferson River. They would need the boats for their trip home. They couldn't afford to lose them in a wildfire. Then they started across the Bitterroot Range of the Rocky Mountains. A Shoshone guide named Old Toby led the way.

The going was tough. The route was rocky, steep, and slippery, for the season's first snow had already fallen. Even the sure-footed mountain ponies had trouble staying on the trail. Sometimes the trees were so thick that the horses could barely squeeze between them.

The trail dipped briefly into the Bitterroot Valley, where the explorers met a band of Salish Indians. These kindly people threw white robes over the men's shoulders and smoked a peace pipe with them. The expedition camped in the valley at a place they named Traveller's Rest. Then they trudged back up into the mountains, following the Nez Perce trail that Cameahwait had warned them about. Today this route is known as the Lolo Trail.

The Lolo Trail was as bad as the Indians had said. It crossed a narrow, jagged ridge that plunged seven thousand feet down to the thunderous Lochsa River. The party had nothing to eat but dried berries, an occasional scrawny grouse, and tallow candles. Finally they killed one of the horses and ate it. The horses were starving too, for any grass that could grow in the rocky ground was covered with snow. The weather grew bitterly cold. Clark wrote in his journal that he was as "wet and as cold in every part as I ever was in my life." He feared his feet might freeze off after all.

President Jefferson had predicted that it would take half a day to cross the Rocky Mountains. In fact, it took the expedition a month. When at last the Lolo Trail dropped down into the valley of the Clearwater River, the ragged, miserable explorers gratefully stumbled out of the mountains. They had left the Louisiana Purchase and entered the Oregon country.

They were greeted by the friendly Nez Perce Indians, who gave them shelter and fed them dried salmon and camas root. The hungry travelers wolfed down the food—and immediately became deathly ill. Maybe they had stuffed too much too quickly into their shrunken bellies. Maybe the salmon had gone bad. Whatever the reason, the whole expedition was doubled over in agony for days.

The Nez Perce told the explorers they could reach the Columbia River by floating down the Clearwater. So all the men who were well enough to work started making dugout canoes. The party left its horses with the Nez Perce, who promised to take care of them until the explorers returned—if they returned. On October 7, the expedition launched its canoes into the Clearwater River, bound for the Pacific Ocean.

# Downstream to the Pacific

As the swift Clearwater River swept the little canoes downstream, the explorers whooped and cheered. For the first time since leaving St. Louis, the current was working for them instead of against them.

"This is more like it!" crowed Sergeant Patrick Gass. "I could learn to like this kind of river travel." But when the canoes reached the first big rapids, the merriment came to a sudden halt. Sergeant Gass's canoe crashed into a rock, ripping a hole in the side. Freezing water poured into the canoe and sank it. Several of its passengers couldn't swim, and there were no life jackets in those days. The men had to cling to rocks until the next canoe could rescue them. This was only the first of many dangerous rapids. For the next month, the explorers spent most of their nights drying out supplies and repairing canoes with pine pitch.   At the present border between Idaho and Washington, the Clearwater poured the canoes into the Snake River. The Snake was twice as big as the Clearwater, and so were its rapids. Had it been earlier in the year, the expedition probably would have portaged around many of these falls. But winter was coming. The party couldn't afford the delay. Fortunately Cruzatte and Labiche were expert river runners. They would study each rapid for an hour or more, memorizing every rock and whirlpool. "What do you think?" Clark would ask, shouting to be heard above the pounding water. "Can you lead us through?" Cruzatte would turn around with a wild grin.

*"Capitan*, this one will give us tales to tell for the rest of our lives. Let's run it!"

As they lurched and tossed down the Snake, the explorers passed by one Indian village after another. The villagers were alarmed to see these strange travelers. Some thought they were creatures from the sky. But once they saw Sacagawea and her baby, their suspicion changed to friendliness. They knew no war party, human or alien, would travel with a woman and child.

Since game was still scarce, the explorers depended on the river Indians to sell them food. Most of the men couldn't stand to eat the pounded salmon that the Indians lived on. So they bought dogs to eat—much to the amusement of the Indians. For the first time in months, they had plenty of food, although they weren't particularly fond of it. "Dog meat!" Clark would grumble. "I think I'll go back to eating candles."

Near the present-day city of Kennewick, Washington, the expedition entered the mighty Columbia River. Two weeks later they came to the Cascades, a deep gorge that forced all the water of the Columbia into one narrow channel. Even Cruzatte and Labiche did not want to brave this fast, churning water. The men had to portage by sliding their canoes over poles from one rock to the next. Indians helped them by carrying their heavy gear on horseback.

Beyond the Cascades, the landscape changed. Stands of evergreens replaced the open plains, and steep rock walls plunged down to the river, sometimes leaving no place to camp. At times the men had to pile rocks in the water to sleep on.

# The Pacific at Last!

One foggy morning in November, the men awoke to find their camp flooded. Lewis tasted the water that sloshed around his bedroll. It was salty! The tide had made the river rise. They must be near the ocean.

That afternoon, when the thick fog burned off, they saw it. "Great joy in camp," Clark wrote happily in his journal. "We are in view of the ocean, this great Pacific Ocean which we have been so long anxious to see. And the roaring or noise made by the waves breaking on the rocky shores . . . may be heard distinctly."

They had done it. They had crossed the continent, covering some four thousand miles. Though they wouldn't know it for months, they had beaten the British in finding a route to the Pacific. On December 3, Clark carved his name into a large pine tree near the ocean. He added the words, "By land from the U. States in 1804 & 1805."

By Christmas Day, the men had built a fort and cabins for their winter stay. They called it Fort Clatsop after a nearby Indian tribe. They celebrated Christmas by singing carols and exchanging what gifts they could find—Indian baskets, handkerchiefs, tobacco. Joseph

Whitehouse made the captains new moccasins. Sacagawea gave Clark, who had become her friend, twenty-four beautiful white ermine tails. The best Christmas gift of all, though, was to be warm and dry, away from the howling wind and rain.

Day after cold, wet day passed by with little to break the monotony except hunting trips and occasional visits from the Clatsop Indians. One day the Clatsops brought news of a whale skeleton several miles from the fort. Some of the men organized a party to go and see this wonder. Sacagawea wanted to go with them, but the men turned her down. For the first time during the long trip, the Indian woman complained. "I have come a long way," she said, "and I have not even been allowed to explore the great water yet. Now you won't let me see this monstrous fish either. This is too hard." The men got the message. Sacagawea saw her whale.

In March 1806, the expedition headed back home. Before leaving, the captains wrote a short account of their journey. They left several copies with their friend Comowool, the Clatsop chief, and they nailed another copy inside their cabin at Fort Clatsop. If something happened to them on the way back, at least there would be a record of their trip. Maybe someday it would fall into the hands of Americans.

# The Return Trip

The expedition struggled back up the Columbia River. The river, swollen with spring runoff, was twelve feet higher than when the men had descended it in the fall. They finally had to abandon the canoes and trade the last of their merchandise for horses from the Walla Walla Indians.

In May, they reached the Nez Perce village where they had left their horses. They stayed there for a few weeks, waiting for the mountain snows to melt enough so that they could cross. "That icy barrier that separates me from my friends and country," Clark wrote in his journal, "is yet white with snow many feet deep."

The men dreaded crossing the Lolo Trail again, but they were anxious to get home. Their impatience drove them to enter the mountains too soon. They almost got lost in the deep snow and were forced back to the Nez Perce village to find guides. Once again, hunger and cold accompanied them over the Lolo Trail. But this time they were rewarded for their efforts when their Nez Perce guides led them to a natural hot springs. There the explorers had their first hot bath in two years.

When the expedition reached the Bitterroot Valley, it split into two groups so that the men could explore more territory. They were somber when they parted company on July 3. They had been through so much together. Would they ever see each other again? "Goodbye!" they called as they went their separate ways. "Good luck!"

Clark and his party went southeast to where they had sunk the canoes near Jefferson's River. They retrieved the boats and paddled down the Jefferson to the three forks. From there, Sergeant Ordway and nine men left Clark's main party and took the canoes back down the Missouri. They were to meet Lewis's party at the great falls of the Missouri.

Clark and the remaining twelve, including the Charbonneau family, went overland to the Yellowstone River. Near the present-day town of Park City, Montana, they built new dugout canoes and quickly floated the almost eight hundred miles to where the Yellowstone meets the Missouri. On the way, Clark carved his name on a tall rock and named it Pompey's Tower after Sacagawea's baby. Today it is known as Pompey's Pillar.

Lewis and his nine men had a more eventful trip. They took a shortcut overland on horseback to the great falls. Six of the men stayed at the falls to dig up the supplies they had buried there the previous summer. Lewis and the other three men explored Maria's River to its northernmost point. From there they could see the peaks of today's Glacier National Park.

On their way back to the Missouri, Lewis and his three companions got into a fight with a band of Blackfeet Indians. They had had an uneasy meeting with the Indians but had camped the night with them. At dawn, they woke to find the Indians stealing their guns and scattering their horses. In the confusion that followed, two Indians were killed. Lewis was horrified. They had managed to avoid fighting with Indians for the entire trip, and now they had killed two. But there was little time for remorse. The rest of the Blackfeet had ridden off, probably to gather a war party.

Lewis and his men made a desperate two-day dash for the Missouri, running their exhausted horses day and night. When they finally reached the river, they heard shouts and rifle shots. They looked upstream to see their friends paddling down the river! It was Sergeant Ordway and the party that had separated from Clark at the three forks, plus the men of Lewis's party who had opened the cache. "Good timing!" Lewis shouted as he and his men leaped into the canoes. Soon the fast current of the Missouri carried them out of reach of the enraged Blackfeet.

On August 7, the canoes reached the Yellowstone River, where the men found a note from Clark saying that he had gone on down the Missouri. For five days they quickly paddled down the river, trying to catch up with Clark's party. Along the way, Lewis was shot in the

thigh by Cruzatte, who mistook him for an elk as they hunted in the thick willows along the river. The wound was so painful that Lewis stopped writing in his journal and left it to Clark to record events of the rest of the trip.

Despite Lewis's injury, the party continued down the Missouri. At last they rounded a bend to see their friends camped on the shore. What a reunion they had! Cruzatte tuned up the remaining strings on his battered fiddle, and the men sang and danced and told stories of their adventures long into the night.

# The Home Stretch

On August 13, the expedition started on the last leg of its journey. The explorers fairly flew down the Missouri now. High water and the men's longing for home gave them wings.

When the men reached the Mandan villages, they said goodbye to Charbonneau, Pomp, and Sacagawea. They knew they owed a great deal to this quiet Indian woman—maybe even their lives. Not only had she helped them find the Shoshones and bargain for horses, but she and her baby had been their peace symbol. Sacagawea had shown strength and courage throughout the trip, and she had earned the men's respect.

Below the Mandan villages, the expedition began meeting boats coming upstream to trade with the Indians. Boat traffic had increased since the expedition's departure in 1804. Already, trappers and traders were beginning to follow the trail the explorers had blazed. The traders were thunderstruck to see the ragged little bunch of explorers paddling down the Missouri. Many people had long since given them up for dead.

John Colter left the expedition when he met two trappers looking for a guide to the Yellowstone country. "Guess the mountains got into my blood," Colter said as he shook hands with his friends. He was to be the first white man to see the spectacular geysers and mudpots of today's Yellowstone National Park.

News of the expedition's return traveled down the Missouri like wildfire, passing from boat to boat. When the men paddled into St. Louis on September 23, 1806, flying their tattered flag and firing a salute to the town, they found the whole town waiting for them on the riverbank to give them a hero's welcome.

They were home at last.

# The Race Is Won

The Lewis and Clark Expedition changed the course of American history. By finding a route across the continent, the explorers played a major role in securing America's claim to the land west of the Rockies. Had they failed, Americans who live between the Rockies and the Pacific today might be Canadian or British instead!

As it turned out, the route Lewis and Clark found was too difficult to be the Northwest Passage President Jefferson had hoped for. Still, the expedition paved the way for the opening of the American West. Where Lewis and Clark led, fur trappers and traders soon followed, guided by the captains' careful maps and journals. Behind the traders and trappers came miners, farmers, and ranchers. Eventually eleven new states were carved from the country Lewis and Clark explored: Kansas, Missouri, Illinois, Iowa, Nebraska, North Dakota, South Dakota, Montana, Idaho, Washington, and Oregon.

If Lewis and Clark could come back today and see the land they explored, they would barely recognize it. Most of the prairie has been plowed or paved. Great cities stand where cottonwood groves once did. Bison no longer turn the prairies black with their huge numbers—millions were slaughtered during the nineteenth century. The great grizzly bear has almost disappeared—only a few hundred still survive in the lower forty-eight states. The great falls of the Missouri and the thundering rapids of the Columbia have been drowned by power dams.

But thanks to conservation, a few areas still look the way they did to Lewis and Clark. The White Cliffs of the Missouri, which reminded Lewis of fabulous pedestals and pyramids, are protected by the Wild and Scenic Rivers law. Portions of the magnificent Rocky Mountains are preserved as wilderness areas. Many other areas deserve to be protected as examples of the American West as it once was. If we act now to save these areas, there will always be a place for high adventure, just as in the days of Lewis and Clark.

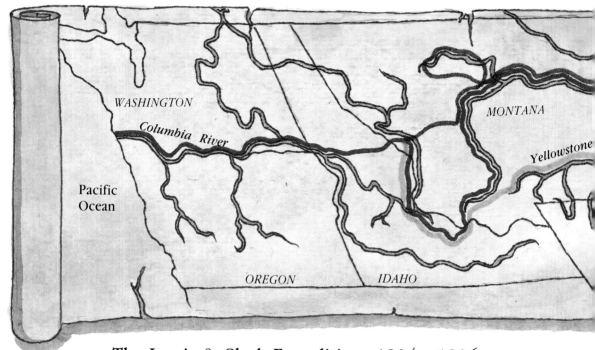

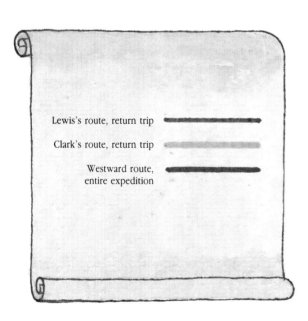

The Lewis & Clark Expedition, 1804 - 1806

Lewis's route, return trip

Clark's route, return trip

Westward route,
entire expedition

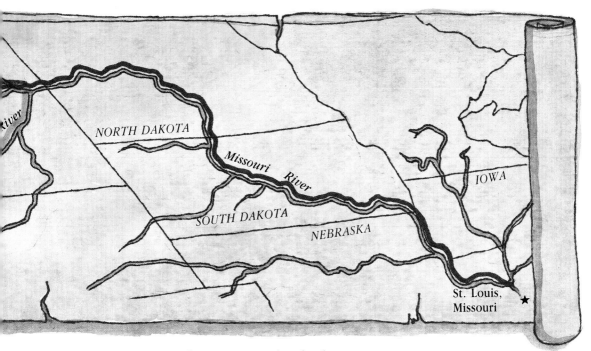

# In the Footsteps of Lewis and Clark

Much has changed since Lewis and Clark made their epic journey across America. Fortunately, a few areas still provide a glimpse of the wild country and wildlife that Lewis and Clark encountered, and many locations feature excellent museums and displays about the expedition. You can trace the path of Lewis and Clark and learn more about their journey by visiting the following places:

*MISSOURI*

**History Museum**
Missouri Historical Society
Jefferson Memorial Building/
Forest Park
St. Louis, MO 63112-1099
(314) 361-1424

**Museum of Westward Expansion**
11 N. Fourth St.
St. Louis, MO 63102
(314) 425-4465

**Lewis & Clark Center**
701 Riverside Dr.
St. Charles, MO 63301
(314) 947-3199

*NORTH DAKOTA*

**North Dakota Heritage Center**
612 E. Boulevard Ave.
Bismarck, ND 58505
(701) 224-2666

**Fort Mandan Replica**
c/o McLean County Historical Society
P.O. Box 398
Washburn, ND 58577
(701) 462-3789

**Lewis & Clark Trail Museum**
Alexander, ND 58831
(701) 828-3595

*MONTANA*

**Upper Missouri Wild &
Scenic River Visitor Center**
1718 Front St.
Fort Benton, MT 59442
(406) 622-5185

**Giant Springs State Park**
4600 Giant Springs Road
P.O. Box 6609
Great Falls, MT 59406
(406) 454-3441

**Gates of the Mountains Boat Tours**
P.O. Box 478
Helena, MT 59601
(406) 458-5241

**Montana Historical Society Museum**
Memorial Building
225 N. Roberts
Helena, MT 59601
(406) 444-2694

**Lolo Pass Visitor Center**
c/o Powell Ranger Station
Clearwater National Forest
Lolo, MT 59847
(208) 942-3113

*OREGON*

**Fort Clatsop National Memorial**
Route 3, Box 604-FC
Astoria, OR 97103
(503) 861-2471

*WASHINGTON*

**Lewis & Clark Interpretive Center**
Fort Canby State Park
P.O. Box 488
Ilwaco, WA 98624
(206) 642-3029 (summer)
(206) 642-3078 (winter)

**Sacajawea Interpretive Center**
Sacajawea State Park
Rural Route 9, Box 2503
Sacajawea Park Road
Pasco, WA 99301
(509) 545-2361

*More information about the Lewis & Clark Expedition is also available from the* **Lewis & Clark Trail Heritage Foundation,** *P.O. Box 3434, Great Falls, MT 59403.*

The TwoDot line features classic western literature and history. Each book celebrates and interprets the vast spaces and rich culture of the American West. The following series are written for young readers with an interest in events that happened in the West.

**TWODOT**
An Imprint of Falcon Publishing

## Highlights from American History Series

Highlighted in this series are pivotal and remarkable historical events in the history of the United States. Each book is concise, generously illustrated in full-color, and action-packed—sure to spark a child's interest in our colorful past.

*The Battle of the Little Bighorn*
*The Lewis and Clark Expedition*
*Pony Bob's Daring Ride*

## It Happened in Series

Entertaining and informative, each book is written in a lively, easy-to-read style, and features 31-34 stories about events that helped shape each state's history.

*It Happened in Arizona*
*It Happened in Colorado*
*It Happened in Montana*
*It Happened in New Mexico*
*It Happened in Oregon*
*It Happened in Southern California*
*It Happened in Texas*
*It Happened in Washington*

## Four-Legged Legends Series

Young adult readers will be enthralled and inspired by these true tales of animal bravery, loyalty, and ferocity. Each book features 8-13 stories and is written by Gayle C. Shirley with illustrations by John Potter.

*Four-Legged Legends of Colorado*
*Four-Legged Legends of Montana*
*Four-Legged Legends of Oregon*

To order check with your local bookseller or call Falcon at
**1-800-582-2665.**
Ask for a FREE catalog featuring a complete list of titles on nature, outdoor recreation, travel, and the West.

FALCON®